Meditative Dhyanastha

ध्यानस्थ [Adjective ध्यान √स्था + क] Absorbed in meditation, Lost in thought, Established in contemplation

ध्यान dhyāna [Noun √ध्यै-भावे-ल्युट्] Meditation, Reflection, Contemplation

Ashwini Kumar Aggarwal

जय गुरुदेव

ISBN13: 978-93-92201-16-5 Paperback Edition
ISBN13: 978-93-92201-17-2 Hardbound Edition
ISBN13: 978-93-92201-18-9 Digital Edition

Title: **Meditative Dhyanastha**
Author: **Ashwini Kumar Aggarwal**

Printed and Published by
Devotees of Sri Sri Ravi Shankar Ashram
34 Sunny Enclave, Devigarh Road,
Patiala 147001, Punjab, India

https://advaita56.weebly.com/
The Art of Living Centre

https://www.artofliving.org/

25th April 2021 Lord Mahavir Jayanti, Sarvartha Siddhi Yoga,
Chaitra Masa, Shukla Paksha Trayodashi, Uttara Phalguni Nakshatra
Vikram Samvat 2078 Ananda, Saka Era 1943 Plava

1st Edition April 2021

जय गुरुदेव

Dedication

Sri Sri Ravi Shankar

The one who effortlessly leads us to profound Meditation

Acknowledgements

Exceptionally beautiful Sahaj Samadhi experience.

Front Cover Photo Credits

Photo by Ali Karimiboroujeni:
https://www.pexels.com/photo/drone-shot-of-houses-during-sunset-10643830/

Blessing

Every human being has the need to meditate
because it is the natural tendency in them:
to look for an everlasting joy.
to look for pure love.

We have known comfort before at some point in time.
This is the reason why we strive for comfort.
Meditation is an absolute comfort.

Sri Sri Ravi Shankar

Guided Meditation by Gurudev
https://www.artofliving.org/in-en/meditation/online-guided-meditation

https://www.srisriravishankar.org/live/

https://www.youtube.com/playlist?list=PL480C9CCB94DF5D82

Sahaj Samadhi Dhyan of Gurudev
https://www.artofliving.org/in-en/meditation
https://www.artofliving.org/in-en/sahaj-samadhi

Contents

Prayer

ॐ असतो मा सद् गमय । तमसो मा ज्योतिर् गमय ।
मृत्योर् मा अमृतं गमय । ॐ शान्तिः शान्तिः शान्तिः ॥

O Loving Divine!
Lead us from the shakiness to the firmness.
Lead us from the ignorance to the wisdom.
Lead us from the transient to the eternal.
Peace in our heart, in our body, and in our environs.

Preface

Why Meditate?

So you can EAT.
So you can SLEEP.

an' be YOURSELF.

Can you be in a Meditative state?
Can you be Dhyanastha?

It is profound.
It is deep.
It cannot be stated.
It can only be experienced.

Meditation Dhyan is a happening that needs to be
Cultivated. Cultured. Practiced.
With Respect and Honor.
With Longing and Sincerity.

Then one becomes Meditative Dhyanastha.
It is the highest blossoming.
It is the pinnacle of existence.

Introduction

Are Family and Friends Important? **YES.**
One's Social circle keeps one Alive.

Is Work and Earning Important? **YES.**
One's Work prevents Pain.

What about Guru? **MUCH NEEDED.**
The Guru wipes Guilt clean. Keeps one Fresh.

In the earlier days Lord Buddha and Lord Mahavir taught their devotees that Meditation was the foremost tool. Even after 3 millennia, all over the globe their disciples Meditate and derive immense and long-lasting benefits.

Today **Sri Sri** is the ultimate wizard for anyone seeking to learn and practice Meditation. In his gentle loving presence, one gets absorbed in Meditation fluidly, this is the living testimony of countless contemporary followers.

<u>What is Meditation? What does it do? Do I qualify for it?</u>
Meditation is the Art of Letting Go. It is total complete nourishing relaxation. It provides deep rest to the **Body**, the **Breath,** the **Sensory Mind**, the **Intellect**, the **Memory**; and nourishes the **Egoistic** Self. All **Human Beings** qualify for Meditation.

But school, family, work do not teach it nor emphasize it? Even the medical fraternity or health institutes do not advocate such a device? **Sounds True...But it ain't.** Not any longer. Not in the hi-tech gadget driven mechanized era. Go out and see for yourself. Come to terms with ground reality.

Honoring the Master leads to Meditation

Faith Sincerity Isolation

Faith and Sincerity get you to the ultimate goal

Tranquil **sound** can be an aid to begin with

Have your own personal space for Meditating

Nothing beats the floor for proper posture

Sunset is a good time to Meditate

and nearness to water is absolutely helpful

When to Begin

Undoubtedly college is a great time to begin

Perhaps school is even better to start treading on this path

Since the mind is raw and trusts effortlessly

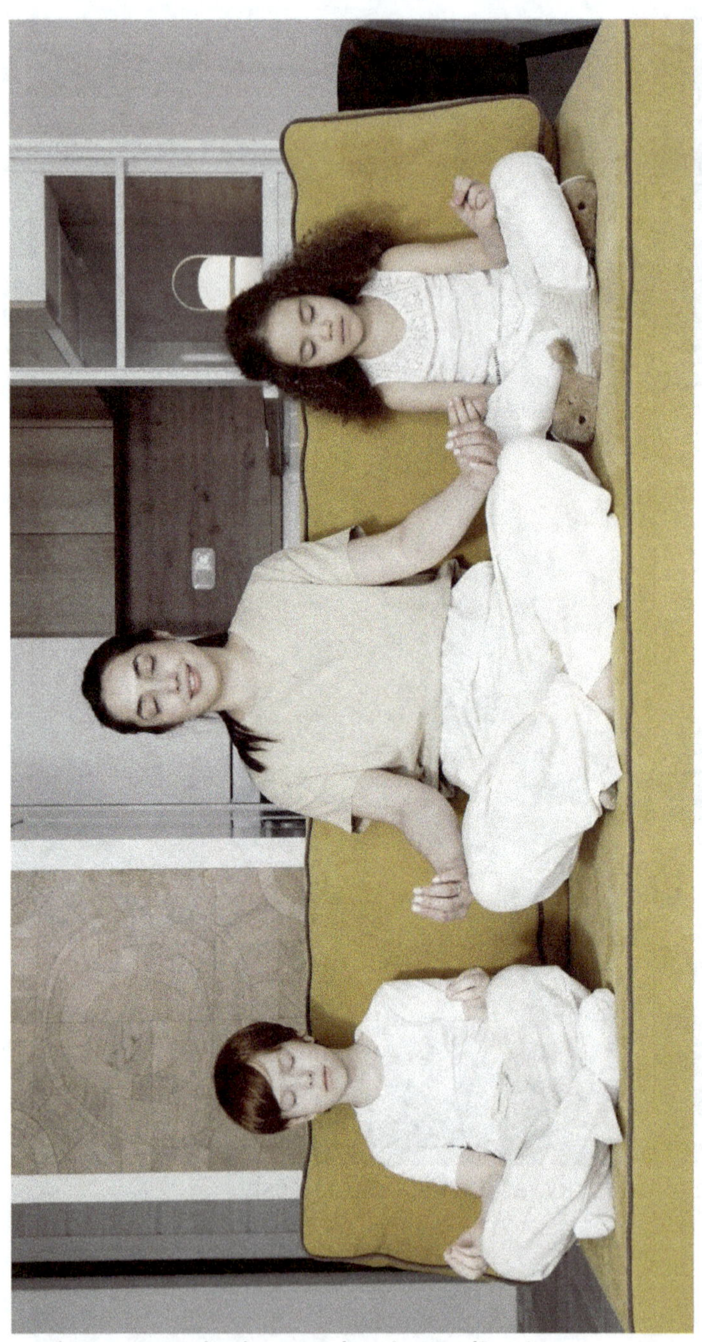

And **Home** is the best to begin Meditating

Entry into Dhyanastha

Upanayanam Yagyopavit is a guaranteed method

Courtesy Vaidic Dharma Sansthan Trust

Sacred Happiness leads to Meditation

Attending Rudra Puja in Sri Sri's presence surely does it

Moments at the Workplace

At work, take your eyes off the paperwork. Look to the side, away from it for a moment; Meditation can happen.

An eureka idea when it clicks and brings a smile to your heart; is a sign of Dhyanastha.

Intense work discussions can end up Dhyanastha

when there is trust and intimacy

a **break** during gardening becomes Meditative

aah! The scent of fresh flowers Dhyanastha

Impromptu Ride Drive Out

Go for an **impromptu** cycle ride along the canal. As your muscles move in tandem unthinkingly, as your thoughts connected to the work plans weaken; know that you are already absorbed in Meditation.

A long drive on a solitary road; and no destination is needed for the state of Meditative.

Usually it happens when one is alone behind the wheel, and there is no shopping to be done, nor any kids to pick up.

Family is being simply available

Just spending a moment with your small child **without doing anything in particular**; results in Meditation.

Cooking can be highly Meditative

And so is just sitting together

or being close to Mother for a **touch and go**

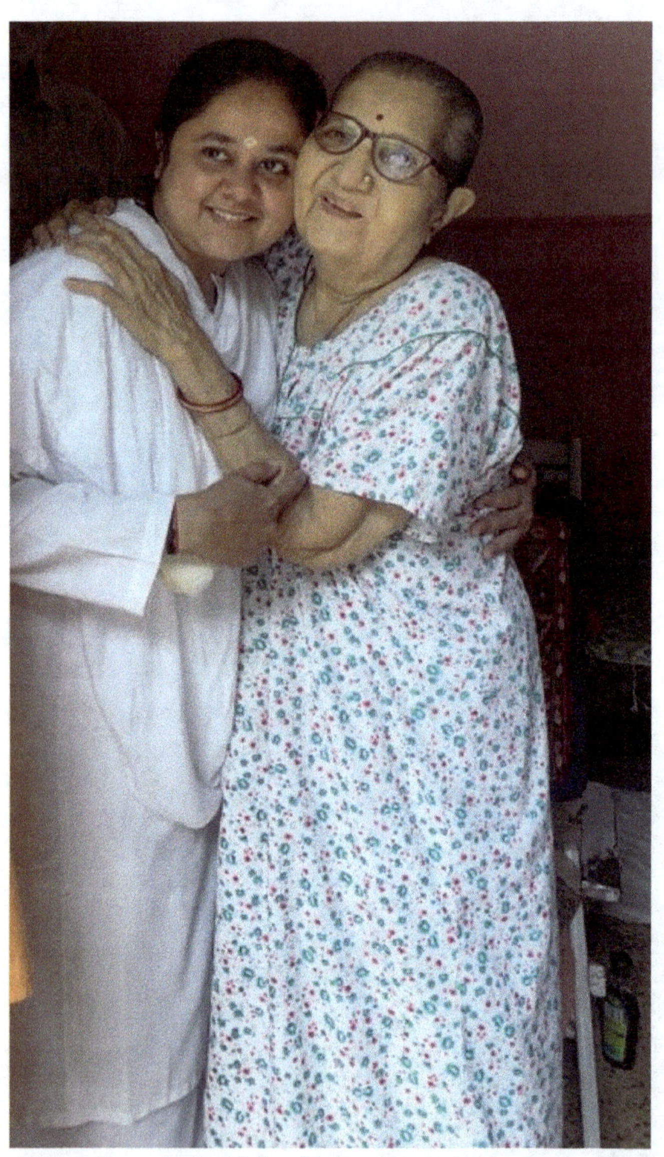
Just a hug; speech is silent

Graceful time with Friends

Playing with a dolphin puts a full stop on all buzzing thoughts; that is Meditation.

Close buddies are meditating often without realizing

Hope wait longing

Good nourishing Meals

Breakfast can start one on the path

if lovingly presented

and filled with Nourishment

especially when fresh and Vegetarian

and eaten together with entire family

Meaningful Dialogue Upanishad

One to one makes sense

Master is Divine

Upanishad happens

in the Master's loving presence

that Upanishad is profound Meditation

in the Lap of Nature

Who can do

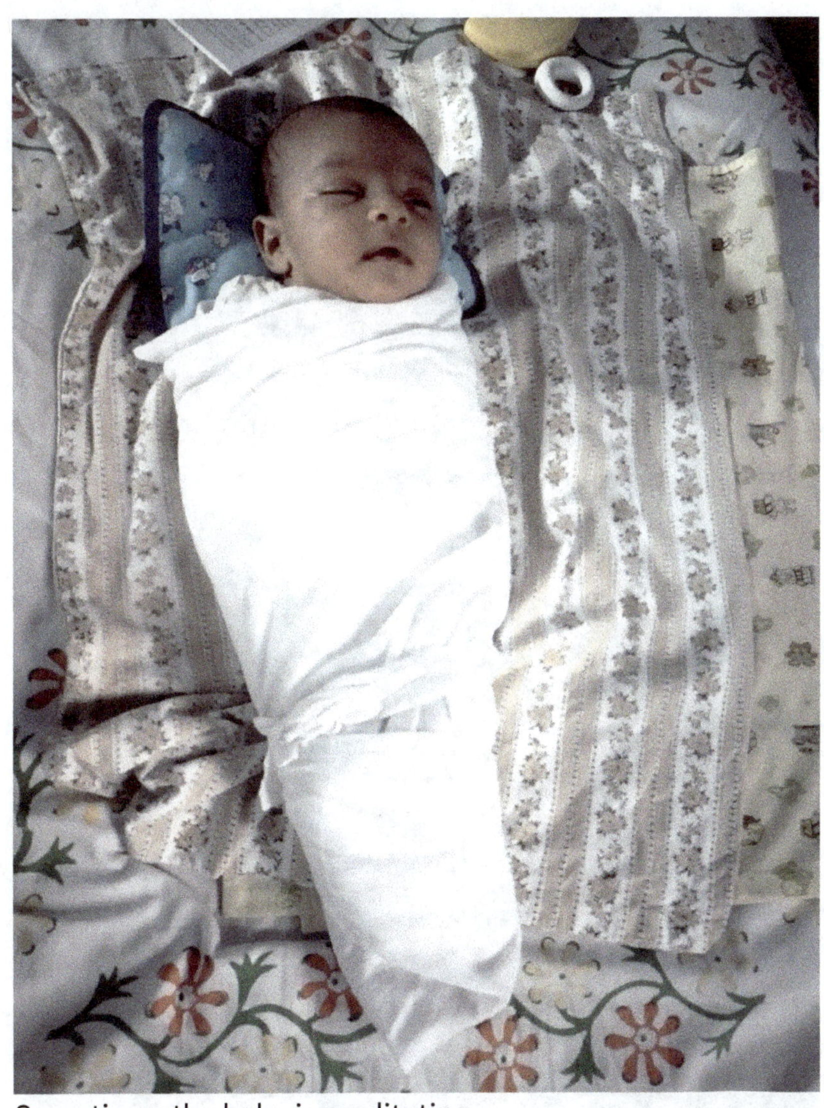

Sometimes the baby is meditating

Singing during divine satsang is Meditative

Music and the Fine Arts

Music and the fine arts lead to Meditation when played with gay **abandon**; not seeking attention; not in competition.

Singing while lost in divine contemplation

Dancing with the Divine is deeply meditative

Crafts; a jolly good occasion to relax and release

Pottery is heart warming and equally engaging for muscles

Painting can get you lost in contemplation

when you put your heart into it

So can creative and digital arts

Posing alone is Meditation

Epilogue

Take time out. For yourself.
It may be the hardest thing. Do it.

Just sit. No plans. Nothing. Stillness. Silence.
Just you.

Few minutes a day. Every single day. Do it earnestly.

सर्वे भवन्तु सुखिनः । सर्वे सन्तु निरामयाः ।
सर्वे भद्राणि पश्यन्तु । मा कश्चिद् दुःख भाग् भवेत् ॥
ॐ शान्तिः शान्तिः शान्तिः ॥

When faith has blossomed in life,
Every step is led by the Divine.

Sri Sri Ravi Shankar

Om Namah Shivaya

जय गुरुदेव

www.ingramcontent.com/pod-product-compliance
Lightning Source LLC
LaVergne TN
LVHW010358160826
845677LV00005BA/1309
9789392201165